WRI

Cover Art by Scott Holland
Illustrations by Carl Brogli and
Aron Ahlstrom
Edited by Karen Sarafin

Inquiries should be addressed to:
Kheper Publishing
P.O. Box 906
Bellevue, WA 98009

Printed and bound in the United States of
America.

DEDICATED TO
MATTRESS, DAVIDA,
PEACHES, AND
MATTALIE

TABLE OF CONTENTS

Common Hieroglyphics

COMMON HIEROGLYPHICS

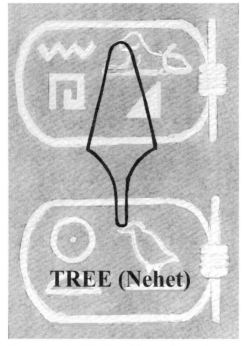

TREE (Nehet)

Represents life, intellectual productivity, and spiritual rebirth. This symbol is a sycamore tree, which early Egyptians believed stood at the eastern gate of heaven.

SCARAB (Kheper)

Symbolizes life, creation, and good luck. The Egyptians used to worship scarab beetles for the way that they emerged from underground tunnels.

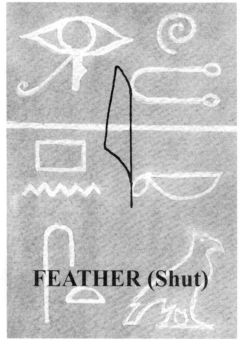

FEATHER (Shut)

Often appears as a sign of Maat, the goddess of truth and order. When in a headdress, it is a symbol of the wearer's identity.

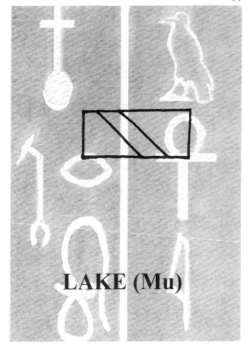

LAKE (Mu)

Refers to a large body of water, such as a lake. Early Egyptians believed that all life emerged from bodies of water.

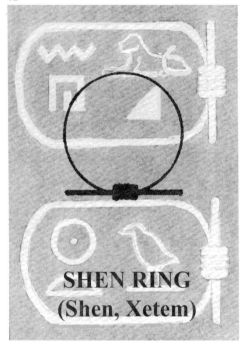

SHEN RING
(Shen, Xetem)

Represents eternity and protection.
The symbol often appears in the
claws of a divine bird that is offering
protection to the symbol beneath it.

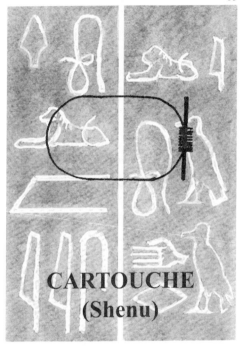

CARTOUCHE
(Shenu)

Holds royal names and writings. It became the standard holder of royal names after the names became too long to fit inside a shen ring.

HORIZON (Akhet)

Often depicts a sunrise or a sunset.
It can also be a visual metaphor,
referring to fire and heat.

LOTUS (Seshen)

Represents the sun, creation, and rebirth. The blue lotus most commonly appears in Egyptian art.

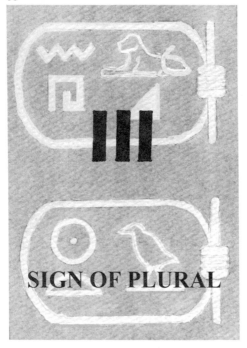

SIGN OF PLURAL

More than one of an object.

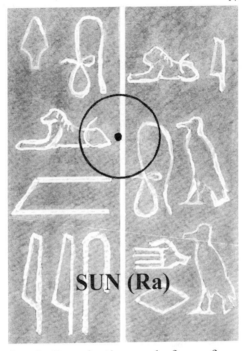

SUN (Ra)

Symbolizes daytime and often refers to the god Horus. The sun was one of the most important elements and many of the gods were solar deities.

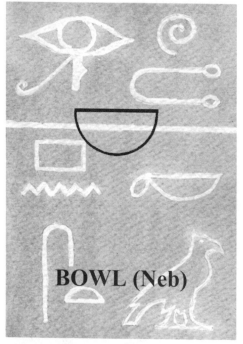

BOWL (Neb)

Represents a bowl or a basket.
When another symbol is placed on
top of it, it can signify "all." Sometimes it is associated with a god or
divinity.

WAS SCEPTRE (Was)

Used as a sign of strength or power.
The emblem is often displayed on
the head of a goddess who personi-
fied a city or town.

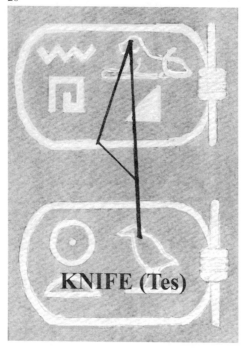

KNIFE (Tes)

To cut or inscribe. The symbol has a
magical connotation, it is often
shown as the tool that destroyed the
sun's enemies.

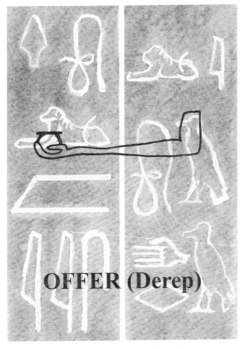

OFFER (Derep)

Signifies an offering. The object
held in the extended hand is the item
that is being offered.

WEDJAT EYE
(Wedjat)

The left eye of the god Horus. It
represents the moon or protection.

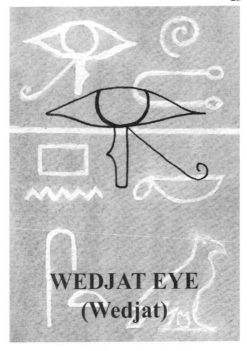

WEDJAT EYE
(Wedjat)

The right eye of the god Re. It represents the sun or protection.

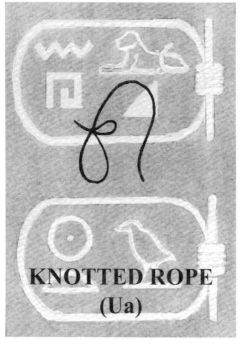

KNOTTED ROPE
(Ua)

Early Egyptians believed that the knotted rope had magical connotations.

MAAT (Maat)

The goddess Maat. Maat was believed to be responsible for maintain-
ing order. The goddess personifies
truth and justice.

HEAVEN (Pet)

Represents heaven, the sky, or the
area that is above a person or object.

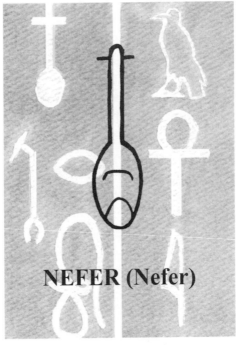

NEFER (Nefer)

A musical instrument similar to a lute. It carries the meanings "good-ness" and "beauty." It can also represent happiness, youth, and good fortune.

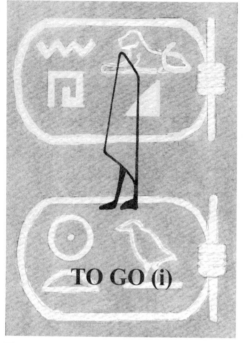

TO GO (i)

To travel or move from one place to another.

SWALLOW (Menet)

A sign of greatness. Egyptians used the swallow to represent a soul that could change into any other form.

VULTURE (Mut)

A representation of the female
principle. It sometimes represents
protection.

ANKH (Ankh)

A symbol of life. It is often used to represent water, air, and other elements that are necessary for survival.

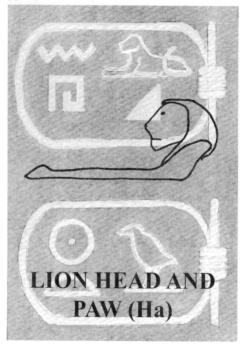

LION HEAD AND PAW (Ha)

The beginning of an object or event.

CHOOSE (Setep)

To select someone or something.

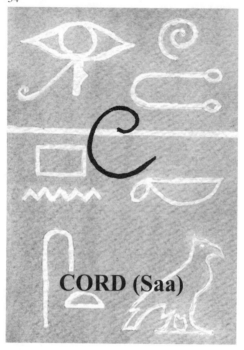

CORD (Saa)

Represents a cord and also the
number 100.

STRENGTH (Usr)

A sign of great strength. This hieroglyphic is often used to represent a person who is very strong.

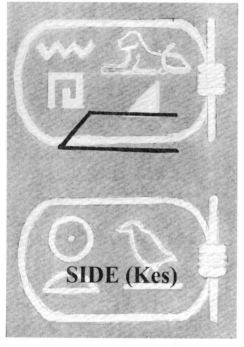

SIDE (Kes)

The side or edge of an object.

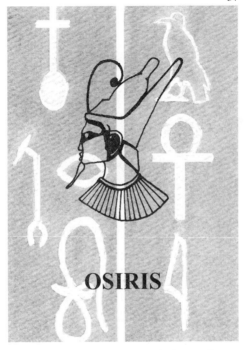

OSIRIS

The god who represented the male productive force in nature. He was regarded as the ruler of the dead and was identified with the setting sun.

KING TUTANKHAMEN

King of Egypt from 1361-1352 BC. Peace was brought to Egypt while he was in reign. His tomb, which contained magnificent treasures, was discovered in tact in 1922.

QUEEN
NEFERTITI

Wife of King Akhenaten from 1372-1350 BC. Her name means, "the beautiful one has come."

**QUEEN
CLEOPATRA**

Queen of Egypt from 51-30 BC. She
is considered to be one of the most
powerful and beautiful queens in
Egyptian history.

THE
ALPHABET
(In Alphabetical Order)

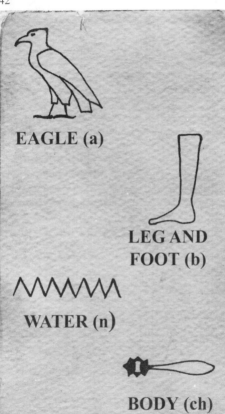

EAGLE (a)

LEG AND FOOT (b)

WATER (n)

BODY (ch)

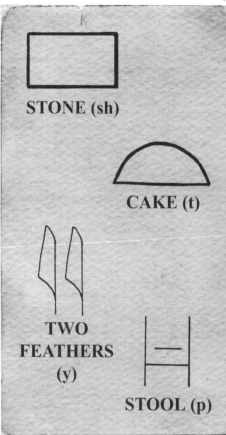

STONE (sh)

CAKE (t)

TWO
FEATHERS
(y)

STOOL (p)

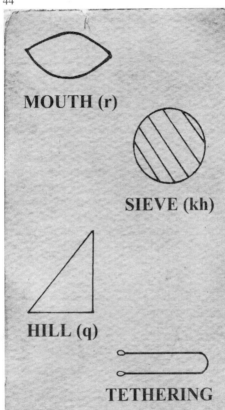

MOUTH (r)

SIEVE (kh)

HILL (q)

TETHERING
ROPE (th)

**SIGN OF
DUAL (i)**

ASP (f)

**SEATED
LION (l)**

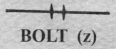

BOLT (z)

FLAT BOWL
(ck)

HAND (d)

CHICKEN
(w)

OWL (m)

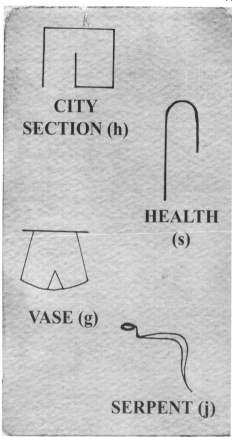

CITY SECTION (h)

HEALTH (s)

VASE (g)

SERPENT (j)